The Rivets

Cynteria McCoy

BookLeaf Publishing

India | USA | UK

DEDICATION

To those that have journeyed through with me without wavering in their standing, this book is for all of you as I pour out the senses of me. It is a book that I only hope you all enjoy!

ACKNOWLEDGEMENT

I would like to give special thanks to my
children and their super love for me

PREFACE

This is the story book for those that need to know that are as strong as they say they are.

Too Close

There are the shock waves of what you thought
would splash you,
Only to know that the rush of the water makes
you too afraid,
How come the sand doesn't feel like it was
meant to dry me up?
When should I get ready to step just a toe in and
feel the true,
It's too much to see as the sun isn't rising
enough,
The different ripples are talking fiercely
whispering to be free,
I'm listening without the intent to hear,
Too many sights, too many sounds,
Stepping deeper and deeper but I can't see,
It's swallowing me up without leaving the
ground,
Not Too close, for I won't make it out

Structured Distress

I called just to receive that one tone,
How does it not be heard?
Based upon what you would tell me,
I chose not to pick up with a fact,
That you would leave me on the other end,
Yearning with discipline as I'm crying out,
Come, come be what I need, I want this,
Didn't I mean to be what you wanted,
Didn't I meant to see you for me,
Wait, wait grab me close, come back,
I'm strong, we can do this,
It's my role to be this loved by you,
But I'm crying because it's done,
Yet you are here to be my wall,
The call is set, I'm still in distress.

Distant Sorrows

It has crossed every shadow,
Just to gaze upon my face,
A mere light that hasn't dimmed,
Shining so heavy on me that I lost that smile,
My eyes are soiled but they won't fall,
It's not here, it doesn't exist,
Creeping in yet so far,
I can't feel it, but I have it,
Dark and closed, empty not whole,
Upon that heart lives,
Distant Sorrows

Actual Worries

Was it really that meant,
Has it gotten this bad this time?
Did I know that it's over?
Only to now lose my mind,
There was no warning to be,
There was a rock and rhythm,
It's a constant show that has me upside down,
Back and forth, forth, and back,
No answers only the worries
To give me all things I lack

Hollow Souls

There was no warning to it
It cam full force as empty as can be
The emptiness, the despair
It's so cold, simple a drift
My spirit says come see
Nothing is inside, just pitch dark
Can you imagine it bright,
No it's so hollow, I can hear my thoughts,
That soul has a hole so narrow,
If only the me inside care to glow

Imperfect Balance

Steady now, we have work to do
Don't teether left or right,
Give that crooked smile a stage,
Where the frown can still have a face
It's a ying yang thing but be careful
The push and pull will make you clear
Clarity has a way to show that
Balance will make a name
But perfection will cause blame
That nothings ever what it seems
Just an imperfect unleveled beam

Limited Love

The sun still shines on those times,
Seeming as full as the rays on end
There was no search for the discovery
That a heart that's so ready
Will be limited and afraid
You carry what's not meant
Only to realize, there's a height
You can't reach, but see
Don't keep going, for there's no further
That love is no longer
It's a limit to limit
No more meant to be in it

Careless Virtues

8

My genre has no beginning
It wasn't that set in stone
I roamed and planted seeds
That always left me alone
I'm here yet wanting more
To know that me trying
Didn't matter for no restore
I made every choice for this
No error of my ways
No misfits
You made my steps order
I'm okay with carelessness
Those virtues flowed like water

Symptomatic Changes

The signs are all there
Pain after pain yet I fear
To admit that is hurts presents it clear
Reality sets the stones and make it so
I'm aware I hurt but it isn't that strong
It stopped yet it repeated
Back again, no wait there isn't
We're to and fro but through
These symptoms left off all clues
The times are changing
But only with you

Pivotal Turns

Open your eyes and vision
Nothing crazy just a sight
Know when and how to go right
Peace didn't appear that way
You were too afraid
Yet you got lost going other pages
I showed you the best places
But you went the left state
Your mind had changed
You no longer trusted that place
I got the map
For you can only see the pivot
That caused this to crack

Actually

Well there you are making problems
causing and wrecking havoc everywhere
No that was you doing what you cared
But my intentions were pure I think
Well actually there wasn't
You made sure that during this time
I don't trust what else I don't see
It doesn't make sense no more
Get out of this space you're in
You are not the end

Reconsiderations

I've thought this over and over
Through and though
My point had back fired
I have taken over this point
It's a magnificent fact
You aren't in any shape
The grace I gave,
Return it

High Sentiments

Disregard what you said
Off with those unpursued words
There that head held high
With no persistent feeling
Just a belonging that this is mine
I'm up as you have put me
Cherishing great moments
As I get this feeling
Hold on to me, give me a notion
That you regulate all portions
Altering all moves
Adjusting my great attitude

Overcoming Hurt

It felt so real but I know not
It felt so strong but not bold
It felt so defining but not meant
It felt so forward yet all cold
I wore it loud and proud
Not to ever bore
That pain came on fast but
I wanted more and more
It gave me what it could
And I let it go for that

Revealing Power

Courage comes straight to you
Get back up again
Open yourself back and take what's yours
it a power like never before
You didn't get there by fault
it didn't just happen
You are awakening
Come forth what you know

Careful Considerations

I bled for this and got nothing
It came at a fast pace only to slip me up
You thought you had me but I tripped on my
own
I saw it yet didn't put two and two
It pierced my plexus but didn't sink through
I came along to see how you can pull it off
Knowing you would fail
Be real steady for those plans have a vail
I will say no after learning your spells

Making It Different

It's all out in the open for all to see
I no longer have what was meant to be
It can become a total a new
The clues and details have their real truth
I can call it for what it is
It doesn't have to be a story now
I'm setting new tones and boundaries
Because everything is so different somehow

Goodbye Heartache

I have carried you for as far as you can go
You have broken me down but I kept wanting
more
It has been quite some time that I have
welcomed you
Oh so freely because I knew it would be through
I have harbored you for safety
Only to know you wouldn't save me
I have set stones to keep you close
Only to know you were froze
But I say it is done and it is over
Those two pieces no longer need closer
It shall mend back to the one
For I gave it to myself and it will no longer be
undone

Peaceful Comings

Joy has shined right on through to me
This breath of fresh air feels too free
It has given me so much strength and power
Come over and stay forever within my timing
I have looked for you and found out
That all those that are coming
Are due to keep giving happy out
It has set its sights on this way
That thing called Peace
Had finally come to stay

Breakthrough Moments

Smiling and knowing I got it all back
The answers that seemed too far away
The structures that were due to be done
The plans that seemed to be canceled
The time that had finally stopped
I went looking and it came out to be seen
The light was ready to be used
It has left me feeling so true too me
That great sense of self
I am who I say I am
There will be no streams of doubt
No more countless fears and tears
This breakthrough was worth every damn hard
years

9 789358 313420